Strands of Luminescence

Poetry Of The Spirit's Quest

Eva McGinnis

Photographs for book cover and interior by Roger McGinnis with cover layout by Alan Halfhill.
Interior design by Heidi Hansen.

ISBN 978-1736684108

Published by Olympic Peninsula Authors dba OlyPen Books
P O Box 312
Carlsberg, WA 98382
olypenauthors@olypen.com

*This book is dedicated to
my beloved twin sisters,
Halina and Krysia,
artists extraordinaire
who have shared
this journey with me,
and to the memory
of our late sister Josie.*

*As well as to the memory
of Seattle poet Paula Gardiner,
my mentor and cheerleader,
to all writers in her sphere.*

*These poems were written
with great gratitude to the
Source of All That Is
for the Gift of Life!*

Contents

Part 1   Luminescent — Emerald Green

Stroke emerald skullcap
of moss on heart rock
sponge up its rich moisture.

Aftermath Of Winter Storms
On The Olympic Peninsula

Part 1

Trunks of alders and fir
ravaged and splintered
like broken femur bones,
scattered alongside the twisted
elbows and gnarled knees.

Several firs wrenched
up by their roots
exposing their fragile tendrils,
like pale private parts
clinging hopelessly
to clumps of dark earth.

Stand of young trees
toppled, intertwined,
stood bravely
against the haughty winds,
stretching and swaying
their branch arms,
struggling to hold onto each other.

Perhaps the old survivors
whispered advice about
withstanding the hurricane
gusts rushing the valley,
"Bend and stay calm."
Not much could have saved those trees
clinging to the waterlogged slopes.

In my private requiem I wonder:
Does a tree feel pain when it's struck down?
When is it really dead?
Does it count, that I see
a tender fiddlehead poised to unfurl
its pale green body among the fallen branches?

Part 2

We clear the bones of my friends
by renaming them "firewood."
My husband saws. I carry and stack
logs to the large pile by the road.
Thumping sound of wood landing
on wood reminds me of
bowling pins striking each other
at the end of an alley,
clumsy days of teen dating.
It makes me smile.

Pushing the wheelbarrow full of logs,
I remember yesterday's conversation
with my friend
in a Georgia hospital;
I wish I could give her a day
in the spring woods.
away from her cancer.

A neighbor and his dog stop by
on their walk down the road
eager to report the large cougar
tracks spotted up the mountain.
We experience the anticipation of
spotting him someday.

Later we spread a blanket
on the most level spot we can find,
eat our sandwiches and split the cookie.
A tiny white butterfly appears and
fusses around us, like my mother used to do.
She would have loved this simple day
with its gentle fragrances,
promise of summer blossoms.
A frog bellows his greeting three times
somewhere in the woods.

January Sounds Beneath The Silence
Mt. Pleasant Woods

God is a friend of silence.
Trees, flowers, grass grow in silence.
See the stars, moon and sun,
how they move in silence.

Mother Teresa

The long-hidden sun alights on my upturned face
like a mother's touch on the cheek of her child,
who has trekked home through near darkness.
I want to believe that the worst of the cold is over.

In shadow, two large footprint-shaped patches of snow,
embellished with pine needles and stray alder leaves,
stand witness to last month's surly storm.
Nearby, maple leaves lay stitched by sequined frost.

Where the sun transmutes the snow,
water seeps up to the spongy surface,
nourishes virile sword ferns
newly liberated from the weight of winter's blanket.

In the deep woods, slick shelf fungi
ring the spruce like twirling skirts.
Bright orange of witch's butter mushroom
silently sings bold volumes of hope.

Downed branches in the clearing
laced together with slender spider threads,
glisten and catch rainbows inside themselves,
weave forest to translucent sky.

On the periphery of my vision,
spirits of forest ancestors,
encapsulated in transparent light orbs,
gently glide among the branches.

When I lower myself onto a downed log,
my thoughts into a sweet hollow,
I can almost hear sap rising
inside moss-covered skins of firs.
The wind, messenger of the river
evokes trills from the throat of a tiny tree frog,
a love song for these woods and for the planet,
awakening codes of light,
bringing me back home.

Morning After February Snowfall, 2019 Olympic Peninsula

Twenty-eight hours of steady snowfall.
Evergreens strain under their thick loads,
frozen branches arc low
into the satin morning sheen.
Pearl-white stillness muffles the creek below.

After snow clouds disperse,
the wind saunters through valley,
lifts powder from topmost branches.
Liberated snowflakes take flight
to neighboring trees or circle back to lower boughs.

As the sun joins in, stronger gusts shudder trees
releasing steamy billows,
micro-jewel droplets shimmer
into shapeshifting clouds,
white dolphin leaping into a donut hole
a swooping bird of prey under slice of sunlight.

Occasionally, swaying branches
release large clumps of snow, which avalanche
onto lower limbs till they plop on the padded ground.
Mists, like gossamer showers, waft
into microsecond waterfalls,
magnificent in their hazy freefall
backlit by the low winter sun.

Carrot-sized icicles drip their sparkling lights
to their own staccato rhythms,
while others crack and spike off quickly,
reckless in their own demise.

By mid-afternoon, the firs undulate with relief,
swing more freely in the updraft of ascending sprays.
Icy clouds parade again on the horizon.
All in motion to prepare for the second storm,
on its way tonight.

Slate Sky

Hangs low over the hillside
where day-old snow still
dampens the air with stillness.

No birds to sweeten the silence
in the shiver of winter.
Clumps of snow catapult
from cedar branches
onto the heads and down unsheathed necks
of a gray couple passing beneath the trees.

Sleet turns their footprints into icy patches.
Balance point between freezing
and thawing slowly oscillates
like toxic lovers who cannot live
with or without each other,
afraid to be alone in winter's bitterness
yet knowing that spring
will bring an end
to the slate gray sky
of their dying love.

The Spiral Universe
Fibonacci's Dream

Double helix sculpting
embryos, shrimp-like
in amniotic brine.

Whorls within sunflowers
fiddlehead ferns
chameleon's tail.

Cyclone vortex
fossil ammonites
chambered nautilus.

Umbilical arch at
moment of birth between
mother and child.

Eddies and spirals
of fingerprints and
cochlea inside ears.

Folds in human brain
hippocampus seahorse
consciousness evolving.

Spiral universe unfolding
in the Milky Way
of all cells.

Wind At Kalaloch Beach

Ocean wind
strong enough to battle tides,
bully and churn charcoal clouds,
keep the earth spinning.

I square my choulders against gritty gusts,
push forward like a mime struggling
with an imaginary umbrella in a wind tunnel.
I sink sideways on the sandy shore
towards the ocean waves,
barely making progress.

With all this supernatural muscle
tugging and pulling everything,
you would think time would speed up.
But instead, minutes hang suspended
like lone seagull flapping bravely,
a pulsing kite
entangled in invisible branches
of luminescent spirit trees
growing close to shore.

Wind whips tears from my eyes,
dries up tear ducts
so no one can see the struggle
is not just with this sand blasting,
but with time stopping
at the shock of your leaving!

Perhaps I need this wind to scour me
raw enough to bury you on this beach
among sand covered crab shells,
crushed barnacles and fallen bird bones
that crunch under my feet, unseen.

Astonishment

Mother bird steps
into my woodland path,
leading me away from
her nest, pretending an injured wing
as if I didn't see through her ruse.
She captures
my admiration
at her bravery,
taking on my giant form
for the sake of her family.

She reminds me of refugee parents
who cross waters in crowded flimsy rafts,
hide in trunks of cars,
stumble over desert sands,
trusting coyotes
who may rob or enslave them
all for their children's survival.
Only to have their children
ripped from their arms at the border.

Yet some affluent others
abandon their offspring
as if they were fish eggs
that know how to swim from birth.

Metamorphosis

> Peace is a delicate plant.
>   Father Aidan Troy

The swamp lantern glows golden
in the spring mud and shallow creek bed,
its dominant skunk smell
warming the patches where snow lingers,
a harbinger of renewal.

Hard-won Peace is like that.
When the urge to claw for revenge
raises the hair on the back of the neck,
the peaceful warrior walks away calmly
blessing the one who curses him.

Peace, like the resolve of the delicate crocus
to push its purple petals to the sun,
lives, when the anger and fear
in the enemy's eyes turn to forgiveness.

A beacon of transformation,
it makes resurrection possible.

Spring – Then And Now

I have read that trees send messages
to each other on the wind.
In my neighborhood, this late March week,
they must have all agreed -
Ready. Set. Send out shoots, now!

How does it happen?
Rough branches on my apple tree
spill out clusters of angel-pink blossoms,
burst into leaves –
tender in new greenness.
As a child, I broke up sticks looking
for the flowers inside, certain I had
only to find the right ones.

What about the pussy willows?
Where did all that fur come from?
Had the ground been collecting
lint from the air all winter
to sprout such little tufts?
As a child, I stroked my cheeks with them
dreaming these were true magic wands.

Can you fathom those lilacs?
They must have simmered perfume
in some underground pockets of my backyard,
at the ready to spray it now
so generously into the breeze.
As a child, I smelled the ground
beneath the giant lilac bush,
searching for secret purple juices.

Today I look at the luminous backdrop of sky
from under the bouquets
of redbud tree blossoms.
The wind, a lover, embraces us.
A petal falls past my shoulder,
a whispered benediction
of miracles I will never understand.

There Will Always Be Weeds

There will always be weeds
to be pulled,
resistant, spiny,
overabundant,
demanding my bent back
as they choke
delicate strawberries.

I have waited
too long this spring
to assert my authority.

Now I strain and yank
with gloved hands
and trowel.

They mock me
letting me have their heads
but not their roots,
though I pit my strength
against their stubbornness.

Blackberry vines defy my efforts
with their underground passages.

I covet the bulldozer
my neighbor used on them
in her desperation.
The succulent leaves of
the dandelions harbor
a family of slugs,
I squeamishly toss them
into my weed bag.

The puffs are pleased
to be set free,
some clinging to my hair.
Sometimes I wonder
if I don't plant more weeds
than I pull, when my slightest
touch releases their seeds
into the soil
I have just cleared.

I suppose there will always
be weeds.

Lone Duck In Wetlands

Last week,
fussy and clucking,
she was surrounded
by eight fuzzy chicks.
They barely kept up with her
as they jostled each other, noisily,
while she steered them away from
my shadow which stretched
to the water's emerald edge.
I marveled at her marshalling style.

Today, she is alone,
on the broad tree stump
in the middle of the boggy pond,
perched one-legged,
head tucked into her feathers
like a yoga master balancing
her low-slung body
in perfect pose.

I zoom my camera lens
to search for her little chicks.
I wait and scan again and again.
But none appear.

I check for the nonchalant heron
who often stands in the reeds
on the other side of the water.

Did she scoop the ducklings
to take to her babies' nest?
She is not there today.

I also suspect ravens
whom I witnessed
harassing another mother duck
and her klatch of chicks
at low tide of the bay two days ago.
I had intervened there, momentarily,
shooing the ravens away from the chicks.

I'd like to pretend
that instead of an early demise,
these ducklings were a fast-growing breed
that flew from home,
too quickly, perhaps,
leaving her standing on her one mother leg,
to catch up on her sleep.

In her stillness
is there grief or resignation?
Do her bird dreams protect her?
Her instincts absolve and reassure her?

Perhaps my sadness for her children
is my own sleepless worry
over my lone chick,
flown, so young,
to a distant pond.

A cool breeze envelopes me
like my mother's whisper.
I feel her presence
and sigh with understanding,
this is how my mother felt at my flight too.

I am not alone,
and in that, there is peace.
I nod my thanks to the lone duck
as she lifts her head
and stretches her wings,
the sun at our backs.

Forest Magic – Mt. Pleasant
Eternal July

Shadows make light show.

Anne Lamott

Weary of city soot I left behind two hours ago,
I stumble on a speckled rock
along the wooded path to the Big Tree.
It leaps into the air – a frog.
I bend down to apologize.

While nearer the ground, I observe
a newly erupted mushroom
standing on its one thin leg,
headful of dirt and needles.

In a sunny spot along the trail,
a curved stick slithers away as I approach.
This time I sidestep quickly,
but the snake retreats even faster
into the underbrush. Not far, a thistle
sports a pink flower adorned
with a hovering bee.
I photograph the bee, which I would
have chased away in the city.

Along the path there are openings where
I hear the echoing rush of the river
in the valley. I play with choosing to hear
its music first as foreground then as background.
I'm thrilled that it's not the dull roar of city traffic,
which I used to filter by pretending it was a river.
Otherwise I would go crazy with its drone.
Here my river holds many songs!

When I reach the clearing, I spread my blanket,
remove my boots and socks,
gingerly stepping on moist dirt.
I watch my toes scoop up soft pine needles.
I relinquish control to the "small animal"
of my body. I am quickly on all fours,
stretching, then on my back
and my hands open towards the sun.
When my mind quiets,
I pull out my journal and write
away my disappointments and
fill up on gratitude for this moment.

On this mountain I feel nurtured
by the sky and wind, which can conspire
to birth rain clouds from pure blueness
in under an hour. This day an angel cloud
floats by and leaves me blessed.

On the way back,
I see the split second leaps of a wild rabbit
across my path and the quick flicker
of the deer's tail as she warns
her two fawns of my coming.

All three disappear completely
into the thick underbrush in a breath's time.
I stand blinking with disbelief.

I follow after them, but the third inner tree
stops me, with its signage of stripped bark
and encircling deep claw marks. My friends
warned me that both bears and cougars have
been spotted nearby this summer. Here are
their glyphs. I put my fingers in
the deep groves and trace them down the tree
in awe of the strength that carves into living wood.
But I venture no further.

Back on the path,
I breathe in the forest magic,
with creatures that shape shift
and messages strewn
in rocks, sticks and sky.

Crystal Hot Springs

Journey to the grotto,
a pilgrimage to a shrine.

Hiking deep into virgin forest,
I step into the stillness of an
ancient grove of firs,
reverently root myself to their strength.
Renewed, I follow the trail
along the steep river bank,
gazing at thundering falls
and massive moss rich rocks
painted deep green by mists.

City blindfolds slough off,
serenity seeps into my bones
allowing me to see
tho wonders of humble mushrooms,
drink musk rich air.

Framed by delicate maidenhair ferns
the hollow in the mountainside
could easily be missed, if not for
the steaming pool at its opening,
quickly disappearing
into stream, joining river.

Alone here this damp morning,
I cannot wait any longer.
The sweaty hike makes my clothes
unbearable and somehow profane.

Tentative steps on moss-covered rocks,
a climb over the manmade ledge
of large stones forming a sitting pool,
I smoothly slip into the bubbling cave.
The water makes room for me
as if I had always belonged there.

I savor the mineral rich silence
in the womb of the earth, generous
with her warmth and lushness,
closing my eyes and sinking into
the steamy softness, blissful.
Coming up, a sheen of tiny bubbles
glistens on my body,
air-laced barnacles.

Too soon I hear laughter
of eager pilgrims approaching.
I seek refuge in the far
recess of the cave.

Lighting a candle, I explore the cavern,
stepping gingerly on sharp rocks,
the triangular ceiling closing in.
I'm not quite able to stand straight.

Each step finds the water hotter
until I reach the effervescent source
too blistering
for more than a momentary caress.
Turning back, I sit on a shallow rock,
placing my candle on a ledge.

Candlelight evokes holy space intensity.
As I envision my own sweat lodge purification,
images of recent crises flash quickly;
I release them with deep sighs,
pray for wisdom and peace.

A presence seems to be at my side
reassuring and enfolding me,
candlelight grows brighter
as tears mingle with sweat.

I emerge before others enter,
grateful for the privilege
of breathing in the mother's holy space.

Finding a cool spot near the waterfall
to contemplate my experience,
caressing the earth with my hand,
I catch the reflecting sparkle of
a tiny crystal between my fingers!

Carbon Glacier
Mt. Rainer

Ancient sculptor
of volcanic valley,
tossing boulders from your face
like beads of black sweat
in the August sun.

Dust of volcanic debris
andesite, basalt,
granite stretches over your
dark ice-wrinkled body.

Rocks big as houses
avalanche off the precipice,
having waited a million
years for this ride.

Columns of dense ejected ice
crumble in their descent,
echoes crashing
off the canyon walls.

Melting waters flow
through your icy veins,
then thunder out from
beneath you, as
a grey churning river.

A chilly wind stirs off
your surface, bearing
the smells from the time
of your creation and
mingling with the sweetness
of the hemlocks that surround you.

Is it possible that in the
eons of your existence
you have conceived a soul?

Cape Flattery Watercolor
Neah Bay, Washington

Distant fog blurs Pacific Ocean
seamlessly into the heavens,
so fishing boat appears
to be floating on horizon,
between blue-grey worlds
on this northern-most tip
of contiguous United States.

Tatoosh Island lighthouse shapeshifts and hides
sometimes in foreground then invisible,
with tip of the island appearing
as an open-jawed sea monster
about to devour any who venture too close.

Boats, clouds and distant boulders become
an interchangeable mirage to dazzled pilgrims
who hiked through cedar and fir forest
on a path overgrown on both sides
with salal, salmonberries,
sword and licorice ferns,
heart-shaped leaves of false lily of the valley.

Many tourists, tripping over tree roots
in thin flip-flops, are surprised
to find themselves on high cliffs
rather than on a beach.

A Makah tribe elder
sits patiently on the observation deck bench
marking the farthest safe outcropping,
answers visitors' questions
about wild life, grey whales and plants.
This land, he wearily shares, is still his home.

All the while, white–capped waves
heave and fold in on themselves,
send enormous whorls of thunder
to encircle or engulf giant boulders,
once part of the continent, now isles
jutting out at the edge of the earth,
lone anchors in liquescent sea.

Heaving breakers rumble and churn
relentlessly toward the rocky shores,
retract, then submerge them in foaming brine,
sculpt cliff faces into vast pillars
or shapes like prows of frozen ships.

Two bouquets of purple flowers
grow out of the vertical cliff
visible only to those brave enough to lean
over the edge of the outcropping.

Flocks of gulls and puffins circle jagged cliffs,
noisily claim their homes
in niches and crannies,
or bob in the waves,
diving for food in viscous kelp beds.
Migratory red-billed Oyster Catchers
compete to raise their young on these slopes
capturing then pounding open mollusks.

One lone fir, bent by wind into bonsai shape,
stands guard at the overlook,
a favorite of photographers
and those not frightened by heights.

Other tenacious trees cling to overhangs
in precarious formations, awaiting
their turn for water-logged burials
someday, after storms loosen their roots
and cliffs release their hold
in suicidal slides into the water.

Farther down the coast,
a monolithic precipice
moss-painted with kaleidoscopic
ochres, browns and fluorescent greens,
hides a cave that echoes
with barking of sea lions,
startling and mournful
beckoning to all,
a return to primordial ocean home.

Seastack Sculpture
Shi Shi Beach

You employ eternal tides,
subduction, uplift and erosion,
instead of hammer and chisel,
to smooth your siltstone,
sandstone and conglomerates
into whale fin
or cone-like rudder atop
hollowed-out ledges, jagged giant's teeth,
even a human face profile
if we examine it at the right angle.

We can only gasp from a far ledge
at the moss-covered body
not claimed by land
and not yet part of the sea,
a lonely hybrid creation.

Summer Reflections By Lake Creek
Olympic Peninsula

On the shoreline where the deer tracks stop,
chanting river rocks
entice me with an invitation:

Come closer,
Step in. Stay.

I gingerly slide my feet
into mountain's glacial milk,
let it seep up my bones,
till I stand straight in icy current,
my spine thrilling to its silver notes.

I stroke emerald skullcap
of moss on nearby rock,
sponge up its rich moisture.

Slick black shape of a seal
etched into boulder,
reveals itself beneath the surface
when my gaze softens.

I marvel at the falling leaf
that lands on the crest of an eddy,
spins its way out
then surrenders to flow,
its epic journey
home.

I breathe berry-scented wind
that strokes my hair,
smooths my brusque edges,
gentles the rhythm of my pulse
till I'm open to Spirit's whispers, once again.

Danger, Strong Current!
(Sign upstream from a waterfall in Washington state)

Narrow river shimmers charmingly,
its exposed rocks slippery beneath their moss caps.
But we step on solid boulders near the shore
where our boots hold us solid to the earth.
I take them off and soak my blistered feet,
you seem immersed in rushing peace.
Later, we scoff at the hysterical warning sign.

But add some mist or rain,
a slight misstep on the wet rocks,
legs entangled in the grayness,
current will grab you into the rocky chasm
just beyond the stone bridge
like a downed tree limb
over a thousand feet of spectacular falls.

Danger, strong whirlpools!

I meet you on the edge of my departure.
Strong remembrance of lifetimes together
drew us like the vortex
suction of a fervent current.
You stand proud and solid
in your innocent trust of our destiny.

I teeter and crash in the undertow,
bump into old snags and deadheads,
eddy around jagged whirlpools, for years
tossing in the wounded belly of my fears.

Finally I'm too exhausted,
cry out in surrender, abandon
to the void, like before my first breath.
I know I am dying
as I ricochet over the falls,
a mere leaf tossed and drowning.

When I land on the slippery rocks,
I find I am bruised but joyously alive,
as if for the first time.
You are there, waiting and smiling.
I look into your limitless eyes.
I now understand - our immortality.

Autumn Snapshots

Every day I see or I hear something that more
or less kills me with delight.

Mary Oliver

Two little girls in red sweatshirts
swing in tree branches
like barely ripe apples,
older sister teeters on lower limb,
dangles burgundy sneakers.
I gasp with a mother's instinct
when they jump together
like a flock of birds responding
to a silent shotgun.
The tree gifts the air with golden leaves
their laughter.

Across the street, young bridesmaids in burnt scarlet
gowns dazzling as puffy autumn dahlias
pose for photos on the pier.
A cool breeze quivers off the water,
sends shivers down their bare backs
as they wobble in unfamiliar strapless heels
to avoid the gaps in wooden planks.
Handsome groomsmen willingly oblige
with protective arms around the girls,
thrilled with the need for warmth in such fine company.

Below the pier,
three Morning Sun starfish
stretch abundant scarlet arms
over rocky bottom at low tide,
while a maroon scallop
sensitive to their deadly embraces
hiccups out of the way
rippling the water
on a perfect ruby day in the park.

Harvest Eve At Dungeness Valley Family Vineyard

Madeleines and Regents, luminous green pearls of succulence
nurtured like grape children for their sweetness,
bask and sway in the windy evening's ochre light
while birds and yellow-jackets raid their pendulous clusters,
oblivious to the flapping scarecrow.
The serene tension of meticulous rows of vines,
is tended by earth mother and her retired surgeon husband
with same precise sculpting he gave to faces of children
born with distorted lips, mouths and noses,
whose lives of poverty and superstitious shame
are reshaped to normalcy and hope by his steady hands.

Gregarious harvesters are welcomed for complimentary dinner
by these vineyard parents, with wine from previous harvests.
Extra sawhorse tables provide for thirty plus guests.
Plates are filled abundantly with greenhouse tomatoes
and basil, bean/corn salad, rich salmon casseroles
with berry cobbler for dessert. Grown son leads the blessing.

As meal winds down, the husband toasts his gratitude,
gives acknowledgements, declaring it a successful year.
There is no mold on any vines. I have walked every row.
But if you see any damage, report it immediately to me.
Then directions for the next morning's harvest:
Pickers wear gloves, bring shears. Be careful not to injure
your partners harvesting on the other side of the same row.
There will be gleaners coming through next week.

A well-respected vintner is coming to transport
these rare grapes from the Peninsula of rain and lavender
to crush and age them into precious liquid amber.

The husband pauses, nods to his wife, then faces the guests.
After ten years of all-seasons work tending the vineyard,
we have decided to call it quits. This is our final harvest.
His voice trembles slightly at those final words
as if he too is stunned to hear himself say them.
Husband and wife's eyes meet to steady their resolve.

You're really going to do it?! an incredulous voice cries,
as the room erupts with groans of disbelief and regret.

He nods, but remains silent, still not sure how
they will say good-bye to all they have lovingly built,
from a rundown century-old dairy farm to renovated farmhouse
and giant barn and cultivated acres of pristine grapevines.

It had been a harsh winter, taxing work through the summer.
He needs his aging hands to be steady enough to operate
on the children's faces that call to him from Tanzania.
They choose the path of compassion.

The shattering sound of a chair leg collapsing at side table
surprises all. The stunned guest is helped up, dusted off,
proclaims himself fine. But everyone is shaken that
this is the final chapter of the Dungeness Valley Vineyard.

Blackberry Lover

I am lured by the sweet scented
radiance of wild blackberry
vines, stretching from the water's
edge to the garden's high fence,
heavy with their ripening purple
in the seasoned September sun.

I sample the outer berries,
crush their juices in my lips.

A breeze stirs the clusters
in the center like savory
wind chimes. Slowly, I slip
my hand and pale arm past
the tangled vines
thorny shadows
deaf to the warnings of bees.

My eager fingers caress
the plump berries, carefully
cradling them, delighted
with their firmness,
lingering in their warmth.

But when I draw them
towards me the whole vine
shudders into ambush.
Angled thorns block my escape
and pierce my flesh. I gasp
in outrage and clench my fist.
The sweet fruit
bleeds blue-black stains.

I twist and squirm in my
retreat, and once untangled,
bitterly swallow the pulp
pull out the thorns and
immerse my arm in river
water, washing away
the sting but not
the wounding.

Hurricane Ridge Ice Trees

The ancestors stand
snow encrusted
forgotten by generations,
frozen in their beautiful grief,
statues of petrified memories
no one remembers loving.

Like the Kennewick man's bones
buried for nine thousand years,
it may be your distant descendants
that uncover your true worth,
and sue to get your remains back
to rebury and forget again.

December Bus Ride To Work
South Puget Sound

First sunrise after winter solstice
backlights ancient mountain volcano
in fuchsia,
rims foothills in golden rose.

We glimpse it briefly,
in the moments
we ride above the fog of the valley.
Everyone around us
is hunkered down
into a nap or a book.

Back in gray freeway lanes,
roadside firs with paint brush tops
hold up the dampness of winter.

Rows of street lights soften to haloc
over roar of traffic, rushing to beat
tyrant clocks in city center.

I tug my coat and shawl snugger
around me,
move closer to my husband,
tuck away the mountain vision
into my heart pocket.

Sable Nights

On cold northern nights
I crave moon blooms
of such sweet fragrance
that will encase and cherish
our honeysuckle love
that already endured
six hundred plus moons
despite little deaths
and crossed horizons.
Each morning,
I awaken, renewed,
thirsty to taste
the fruits of our promise,
to grasp together
the possibilities held
in the crackling of fiery dawns.

Part 2   Luminescent — Midnight Blue

Grandmother weaver
spins me into gossamer lights
till I don't know where I end
and the beaded strands begin.

On Writing Poetry

Poems lure me
with mysterious promises
into hidden whirlpools,
swirling me inside themselves.

An endless trickle
of syllables on my brain
taunting moon madness
on the borderlands of emergence.

Drop me into
blue-ice mountain crevasse
where illusions reflect and splinter
frosted ice-glass shatters on stone.

Sometimes, the tributaries of words
slow and smooth into steady cadence,
birthing a poem
capable of sculpting river rocks,
into a landscape of awakening.

Beach Sand Art

Ocean pebbles ground
into chips like black diamonds
strewn by summer tides.

Are they the Mastermind's sketches
for mountain avalanches, river deltas
and spits, even eagle's feather?

May this life force always tumble
inside the incoming waves
and leave behind such treasure.

Beads Born Of Flame

This bead holds day full of sky,
a night of wine black tides,
his steady heartbeats
as he twirls the molten glass
in the fire of creation.

The secret lies in arranging beads
as if unlocking a code.
When the circle is complete,
clasp in place, I run the necklace
across my lips, smooth it over my cheek,
feel its weight around my neck.

I caress the beads like a rosary
whose power can answer prayers.
I am willing to wait for its secret.

Pearl Knotting

The Latin word "bede" means to pray. And as we stitch
our beads one at a time, I hope we can find solace
in this simple and loving repetition that somehow
adds goodness to the cosmic soup.

Beadwork Magazine

Put on your favorite music,
Pachelbel or Vivaldi recommended.
Prepare your space,
placing cloth on table that will hold all your
vials of pearls, beads and tools.

Pierce the barely visible hole
of a pale pearl with fine wire
trailing gray silk thread,
snuggly place a precise knot
with sharply pointed tweezers,
close behind the pearl.

Thread a faceted crystal,
a knot,
a smaller pink pearl,
a knot.
back to the milky pearl.
repeat the mantra again.

At the center
place a large tear drop pearl,
return to pattern.
At the end join
female and male parts of clasp.

Gems of water world,
clear crystals of earth
knotted together into
a rosary,
no matter the order of the beads,
a universe of rose petal prayers.

Broken Rosaries

At seven years of age, I believed
a beautiful beaded rosary
would capture God's attention,
entice him to grant whispered prayers
captured within each smooth crystal.

I begged Mama
for the pale peach rosary
that reflected the altar candles
and stained glass light in our church.
I dreamed it would open heaven.

Mama had little money, even for groceries,
yet she bought that treasure for
my First Holy Communion.
It was my companion for years.

In church we looked like the devout family;
at home Tata yelled and Mama cried
no matter how hard I prayed.
Childhood misbehaviors were punished by long prayers
recited, out loud, in front of a crucifix, on my knees.

As a teen I realized turning into a woman
meant I became "an occasion for sin."
The rosary's chain was broken,
and my faith found a new home.

Though counting prayers became pointless
over the next thirty years,
my love of beads continued to shine.
I made jewelry for my sisters and friends.
But my mother never wanted anything that frivolous,
only wore her gold cross and her religious medals.

When a beautiful pearl rosary appeared in the bead shop,
I finally felt that I was ready to make one.
So as a Christmas present, I beaded Mama a rosary
of pale pink and gold pearls
complete with an ornate cross.
I easily remembered the spacing and order of the beads
inside the rosary.

As Mama's health was already failing,
I wove this last rosary with love and gratitude
for all her sacrifices on my behalf.
I felt a fullness of blessings flow
into that sacred circle.

I urged Mama to touch the pearls,
make them glow with her reverence.
But she preferred to save nice things
for special occasions,
suspicious of anything too
beautiful for herself.

Or perhaps she could not allow herself
to enjoy it because it meant
condoning my maverick ideas of God
outside the Church.
I don't know which one it was.

Upon her death,
we honored all her requests for a religious burial.
I found the pearl rosary in her dresser,
asked for it to be intertwined around
her hands along with her well-worn prayer book,
just as they are in my First Holy Communion photo.

May she find the peace she never attained in life
and know the blessings of Love eternal.

Fossilized

During the war, the Nazi's brutal hands
around Mama's young neck,
trapped her like an insect in sap,
leaving her forever
frightened of any man's touch.

Years later,
she returned to Poland,
bought golden amber
from the Baltic Sea,
its warmth a healing comfort,
the only stone she placed around her throat.

My father scorned anything
she found beautiful, even the amber.
Five decades she fought off his acrid words,
till her heart hardened
blood formed clots,
deadly beads.

A year after her passing
I string together chips of amber,
crystallized syrup of primordial life
reclaiming her legacy.

The Offering

Aleks had seen many of his fellow soldiers die
in his four plus years as a POW. Only a month
after he was drafted into the Polish army on the eve
of Hitler's invasion, he was with the retreating
troops when he was captured by the Russians
after a bloody ambush, where he was wounded.
He and other survivors were traded to the Germans.

It did not matter who the capturers were;
cruelty reigned and kindnesses were rare.
Survival depended on small acts of resistance,
thefts along the way like an extra potato hidden
in a pocket when forced to pick the harvest,
punishable by death if caught,
or a piece of clothing off a fellow prisoner
who died during the night.

Aleks was good at surviving. He had done it
from his poverty-stricken youth; even as his body
was dwarfed by malnutrition, he was a strong fighter.
In prison he watched his young body shrivel,
his feet bleed, hair and teeth fall out,
and lice bedevil him.

Hunger and exhaustion were constant gnawing tyrants
as the prisoners were forced into hard labor
with meager and often rotten rations.

At night they were warehoused in barracks behind
electrified fences. Aleks watched in horror, then
numbness, as desperate prisoners would succumb
to the spell and throw themselves onto the fences,
setting off the sirens. The guards didn't appreciate

the extra trouble of taking them down, and commanded
other prisoners to dispose of the burnt bodies.
He grew to hate the smell of incinerated flesh.

Aleks prayed to live through each day, making bargains
with whatever unseen powers he hoped
could alter his fate. God or the devil, it didn't seem
to make any difference anymore. But on a
brutally cold winter day after a particularly
vicious gun barrel pounding by a guard,
and no food for several days,
he was at his desperate end and began to see the lure
of a quick death on the fence. The look he had seen
in the eyes of others was now in his, and he had
no strength left to fight. He'd deal with God or the devil
once this hell was over. It couldn't be worse than this.

He began the walk, or rather a shamble towards it.
But a hand on his arm stopped him. His friend, as gaunt
as Aleks himself, whispered "I have something for you."
He pulled Aleks back out of the searchlight, reached into
a pocket of his tattered coat and gave him a raw potato.
His own last piece of food, shriveled and dirty.
Aleks didn't understand at first, but took it furtively
and ate it with a raw reverence that fed him a sliver
of hope and strength, breaking the spell of a quick death.

*(Note: Aleks was my father and he and his friend survived
until Allied liberation a year later.)*

A Hundred Thousand Things Abandoned
Dedicated to refugees in my family
and families everywhere.

Scattered debris of a million lives
      shards of frozen tears
      empty snakeskins of broken hopes
      driven by the acid winds of war or genocide.

Hastily abandoned pots boiling over with
      bitter roots stew,
      child's blanket forgotten in haste
      old man's teeth in a cup, wordless.

Fleeing for the mountains of slow starvation
      or drowning waters of overcrowded boats
      no portable roofs over their hearts
      no satchels of diamonds to save them.

A million people no one claims as relations,
      hundreds turned away at the border,
      a thousand deaths a day,
      a hundred thousand things abandoned.

Mama's Chicken Soup

*My mother's quiet presence is subtle
yet familiar to me as a texture of air.*

Diana Abu-Jaber

Even though it's July,
I simmer the chicken on the stove
till the chunks of meat
fall away from the bones.
I dice the carrots into tiny cubes,
like orange baby teeth,
dunk a whole onion into the broth
let its juices leach out, then throw it away.
Just like she did.

She would have insisted
on plenty of her homemade
egg noodles or dumplings
to swivel around in the soup,
topped with chopped parsley.

As children we were permitted
to eat only after grace
and she made the sign of the cross
on the bottom of a thick loaf of rye bread
with her big knife, from one end of the loaf
to the other and back across.
She said it was what her mother had done
as she spread pale butter on the bread.

She was proud of her chicken soup,
rich with floating golden rings of fat,
prepared at least once a week
throughout my childhood,
a symbol of abundance in America.

Now I bless the soup pot on my stove,
quietly steeping its fragrance
into the pores of my home,
on this anniversary of her death.

The Grand Weaver Writes Through Me

Grandmother weaver
silver haired and shoulders hunched,
with fingers stiff from holding,
spins me into her fine woolen yarn.

She has already combed and carded me,
scrubbing out all the dirty fibers
and coarse words, till I am prepared
to be part of her tapestry.

She weaves me into her poems
till I'm stretched taut on her loom,
my back the warp, my arms the weft,
all my sinews showing.

Her daughters finish off my edges
with finely beaded strands
till I no longer know where I end
and the shards begin.

Grandmother weaver
whispers her stories into my half-dreams,
strokes my hair,
challenges me to remember
for another generation.

Jacaranda Tree

Part 1

In a suburban backyard
at the edge of a drought-stricken canyon,
small birds disappear into canopy
become part of quivering leaves.
Some squabble and shove for their turn
at feeders swinging from low branches.
Squirrel scampers on lawn, gathers the overflow.

Hawk swoops
like a windy squall;
birds catch the updraft
lift off in unison.
For a split second
the jacaranda seems
to hover a few inches
above the lawn.
Then the birds scatter,
seek refuge under bushes
down dry canyon slopes.
Tree seems to sink back
as if pulled taut by its roots.
Squirrel disappears.

In a gust of silence,
hawk lands on gray fence,
near the now motionless tree,
a small bird trapped
in its bloodied talons.

Part 2

The hawk steals into my dream
landing on the cold steel railing
of my mother's hospital bed.

Hawk turns his head from side to side
observes her shrunken gray form
sleeping restlessly,
propped by hefty white pillows.
Bruised skin of her hand
pulled taut into a pucker around the
long needle threaded
to bag of dripping fluid.
A clear tube divides her swollen face,
dips into her nostrils.
Another discreetly carries away her waste.
Its smoll mingles with disinfectant undertow.

No one else sees the silvered hawk,
though the nurses' station is just outside the door
and strained laughter spills over the threshold.

Frantically, I search for cover for Mama.
It's too late to move her.
He won't attack what he cannot see.
As he shifts from one claw to the other
I whip off my sweater and shield her face.
He is startled by my movement,
extends his wings.

As he rises, I lunge in front of him
pull aside the curtain to the next bed,
wave him toward the 92-year-old woman
her mouth wide open, unconscious.

"Let her be the one.
Anyone but my mother!"

I spread out my arms to protect her.
but she is sputtering under my sweater,
grown into a heavy maroon blanket
embroidered with birds sitting in a jacaranda.
I pull it off in horror.
She is coughing and choking.
When I look back, the hawk is gone.
I awake trembling, my throat dry with sobs.

Part 3

The next morning, I'm hesitant to visit
Mama in the hospital.
My sister's presence comforts me.
When we enter, Mama is awake.
I'm always astonished at her face,
once heart-shaped,
now distorted into a full moon
by years of medications.

Her cheeks, no longer gray
hold a withered ruddiness.
Though her lips are parched,
her threadbare voice is stronger.
Only the translucent blue eyes remain
as I remember them.

We ask about her night's sleep.
"The woman next to me
screamed during the night.
They took her early this morning
after her heart stopped."

I scan the room
the beating of wings
suddenly in my throat.
I find it hard to breathe
step outside for a few minutes.
There is no sign of the hawk.

When I can speak again with her,
Mama asks me
to bring her a favorite rose,
from the bush
growing by the jacaranda tree.

Stepping Away

My mother's feet are
lukewarm stones
almost lifeless in my hands.
I anoint them with almond oil,
pale parchment skin stretched taut.
I knead hidden lumps like pebbles,
gristle of shoeless years,
the dent between her toes,
where a cow's hoof
once crushed fine bones,
from which she limped for years
in war time enslavement
on a German farm.

If only my hands could infuse the
humble hollow of the arch with vigor,
toes with chubby joy.
If I could cup the heel with soft affection
she might sleep gently tonight.

Earlier I cajoled her into a short walk.
She held my hand
declared it strong
pointed out calluses
I hadn't noticed.
"You surely work hard, my daughter."

I steadied her stumble.
"Mama, you must make the effort
to walk more often."

"I am tired of effort.
Let's turn back,
the sun is too harsh."

Mama's Last Week

Her legs so still under light blanket,
arms unmoving, except
for tremors rippling through the "wounds,"
battle scars from deadly talons
armaments of half-poisonous medicines,
though she has now stopped taking them.
My touch or prayers not equal
to task of rescuing her.

Each day her skin grows
more translucent blue, veins more prominent,
breath raspier and cough more difficult to calm.
I pore my warmth into her hands,
massaging feet, combing her hair,
sponging her fragile face,
white eyelashes and brows,
willing her to stay just a bit longer.

One evening I bring her dinner tray
but a stroke has thickened her tongue,
stolen her ability to talk and swallow.
She speaks her love only through
her luminescent eyes.
She knows it won't be long now
Her husband of fifty-three years,
my sisters and I sing her all the songs
our numbed brains remember.

Around her deathbed
shadows of her parents, younger brothers,
dreams of a sweet apple orchard in Poland
where she was nine years old
singing and dancing around the trees.
They beckon her to leave her grey shell,
swoop in one bright arc into the light.

The Last Photograph

Our mama was not supposed to look like that!
Her toothless mouth slacked open,
as if her departing soul unclenched
all the hinges, leaving this last exit ajar.

Her eyes had been her last haven
as death sauntered through her body,
turning out the lights in each organ and limb,
moving her spirit out like a greedy landlord.
I dreaded closing her eyes,
but pain had sealed them shut.

Mama had been unconscious
since the middle of the night,
her struggle with failing lungs
eased by drops of morphine
while we three sisters sponged
her feverish body, trying to calm
the heat of her fiercely pumping heart.
Unknowingly, we performed
that ancient rite of daughters,
washing the body for burial.
She relaxed into the coma,
her shallow raspy breathing
a mere pilot light,
during that long twilight.

Mid-morning, sister Halina & I
felt compelled to drive into town
to find the funeral home,
choose the white coffin with
angels guarding each corner.
Our sister Krysia was by her side
with instructions to call if her breathing
slowed or changed.

Instead, the pilot light went out suddenly
the moment we stepped out of
the funeral home.
That wasn't supposed to happen!
We ached with regret of brief moments away.

We didn't cover her dear face,
but stared into it, embedding it in our hearts.
Halina and I on either side of the bed
holding her hands, willing our warmth
to keep the final shade of paleness
from evaporating from her face.
She grew no whiter, only colder.

Our father took his turn,
stretching full length over her, sobbing.
Abruptly, he straightened,
asked for the camera. Halina hesitated.
"We have so many beautiful pictures of her,
You don't want one of her like this."

But he shouted "That's my wife and I want
A picture of her, right now!"

I remembered the photos from Poland
of my grandmother in her casket with
the family standing around her.
Perhaps his request was not unusual.
But it was too much to ask in this raw hour of death,
when all our minds were bleary with shock.

But he would not give up.

I propped a rolled towel under her chin,
drawing the blanket close.
But her poor jaw would not close.
A numb part of me hoped she might speak out,
appease his anger and shield us from him once again.
But she was silent, we, her orphans.

I stroked back her thin gray hair
arranged the pillow under her head.
Halina took the picture. He insisted on more.
Courageously, she clicked past her outraged tears.

When it was over, an awkward silence returned.
My sisters and I exchanged looks of resolve.
We would never let him see those photographs
that would be lost in development.

Walking With Her On The First Day Of Fall

On the path to the ancient cedars,
mountain breeze only chooses special branches
to caress, leaving others waiting for the touch.
Hawk alights on topmost branch of sapling,
swaying and listing from side to side,
before departing. He has taken his prey for now.

Earth button mushrooms, innocent but dangerous
glisten beside the path in shady damp nooks,
Indian plum tree festooned in flamboyant golds,
amidst the staid greens of firs and cedars,
comforts me with its splendor.

Maple leaves crunch underfoot, browned
by the dry summer that didn't plan for fall colors.
When we reach the giant cedar,
I almost genuflect with respect.
I can't touch it, surrounded by its children and wind song.
I feel its strength and encouragement.

Turning around, my shadow falls across the path,
propelling a cricket to arc away, clacking.
Its dirt colored body momentarily reveals
inner golden tipped wings.

A white butterfly that leaves no shadow
flutters into the ancient tree.
She is free now and breathes
the luminescent blue air of fall.

Mists Of The Mountains

Spirit of lakes and seas and rivers,
Bear only perfumes and the scent
of healing herbs to just men's fields.

Henry David Thoreau

Gossamer veils, transparent shrouds
mists drape over my tree encrusted mountains,
softening my gaze, muting my steps
whispering of timelessness, soft endurance,
blessing with fine sprays of holy water.

Is this where you walk now, beloved Mother,
free from fear of heights and false anchors?
Do you fly above mists or float inside them?
Will you encapsulate me again
in your watery womb?
Or must I just dream of our reunion
in the herbal sweetness of an imaginary heaven?

EVA MCGINNIS

Part 3   Luminescent — Sacred Gold

Maple sonata of forest mystery
resounds Gaia's heart song.
Sacred grove of the Beloved.

Beads Of Light

It seems only yesterday I used to believe
there was nothing under my skin but light.
If you cut me I would shine.

Billy Collins

When my daughter was small,
she saw her first rainbow
springing from Mt. Tahoma and dipping
behind the foothills in the moments
when it was both raining and not.

We played on the floor
with big red, blue and yellow beads,
grouped them together on a pegboard
into shapes of animals or houses
and, of course, rainbows.
Once she strung them on a shoelace
then twirled them on her arm
like a limp hula hoop, clanking and laughing.

Her gift that Mother's Day
was a necklace of paper beads
rolled from strips of magazine pages,
macaroni patterned with Magic Markers
and Fruit-loops strung on yarn.
"Just like the rainbow, Mommy,"
she chirped as she put it around my neck.

Lost Poems

Poems stalk me like lost children,
gnomes under tree stumps,
fairies swinging from precarious branches.
Like high note bird songs thrilling at dawn
or dark calls of ravens disrupting my peace,
fully formed, but unborn, they beckon to be seen,
acknowledged, taken by their hands,
walked into existence.

When will you have time for us?
When can we show you our treasures, our scars?
Don't ignore us and put us off again.
We know all your excuses,
calls you listen to instead of ours.

Words, like dew drops clinging to tips of cedar branches,
shine with promise to heal these lost children,
bring them in from the rain and comfort them
in alphabet blankets of spun light,
listen, record and bind them into books
and give them life.

Rosebud

The morning light
finds us entwined
like a rose bud,
hugging the covers
around us.

As the warmth
of the sun
coaxes open
the bud
so we
gently unfurl.
Your arm lifts
the quilt,
you awaken me
with a kiss
on my breast.

Your thighs,
tender as the
innermost hollow
of a petal,
release
my legs.
I stretch
toward the sun
to greet
the day and you,
my beloved.

Imagine The Central Sun

Inside Gaia,
as her heart.

When she breathes with fiery passion,
volcanoes erupt
on her salty ocean skin,
or through rocky cones.

When she naps
in coolness,
glaciers scrape
her mountainous wrinkles.
Poles shift at her sneeze.

In cycles of millennia, she is
lovingly bathed in music of the spheres,
the eternal sound of the Source.

Gaia's sighs
birth new creatures;
Spirit into matter.

As her small, but conscious child,
I cannot comprehend,
the billions of years she's lived,
any more than a moth
that lives a lifetime in one day,
understands me.

Still, we all meet
in dreamtime awareness,
where the moth hums,
and I kiss the rosebud's dew.

Labyrinth
A Wedding Poem
(Epithalamium)

Sacred maze of destiny,
we meet at its edges.
Drawn into the vortex
across distances as vast as that ultimate labyrinth,
the spiral Milky Way.

We peer tentatively over star-strewn hedges,
circle cautiously like orbits of planets,
retrace constellations of familiar patterns.

Look inward at self, look outward at self,
eyes seeking confirmation of trust.
Inching and leaping towards love
already destined in both hearts,
letting the years provide the evidence
that the labyrinth is a safe home,
as intimate as the heart
of the Chambered Nautilus
found at its center.

Every moment, perfect,
in its intricate richness
where falling down means startling awake,
illness, a sharpening of gratitude for privilege
of being allowed to walk this journey.

Today, our steps are bold,
hands entwined, rings blessed.
Hesitation banned outside
the rose mandala
of the family's protective embrace.

Eyes no longer averted,
but glowing with conviction
that this labyrinth is,
at last,
the only path,
to the Beloved.

Love Has Chosen Us

This has nothing to do with religion.
It is Biology. We need Love.

Dalai Lama

Love has chosen us
to be the hands, eyes and heart
of unity and compassion
for all our brothers and sisters
seeking the sacred space
of Home
on our Mother, the Earth.

Love has chosen us
to release our judgments
of anyone who wears
a different "earth suit,"
whether on two or four legs,
to offer an outstretched hand,
an open heart.

Love has chosen me
to hear the hope
of springtime
in cacophonous bird songs,
which echo the longing
for Peace, Love and Joy
within my own heart.

Love has chosen me
to witness the unfolding
of Spirit's plan
revealing humankind's
unlimited potential
unspeakable beauty.

Love has chosen us
to be the eyes of truth
hands of support
hearts of Grace,
large enough to hold
the sacred circle
of all sentient beings.

Blessing Of Animals Service At Unity Church
November 2019

After a series of gerbils named Whiskers,
hermit crabs all called Hermie, countless fish,
a Mini-Rex rabbit dubbed Maleeka, who lays
beneath a hand-carved gravestone in our woods,
I am content that critters live in other people's homes.

Early mornings bring the doe and her fawn to graze
on tender daisies and new grasses in our back yard.
The speckled fawn was born in the tall brush by the ditch.
I watch them from above as they flick their ears and tails
but take no notice of me. Just the way I like it.

A neighborhood labradoodle enjoys chasing deer,
stressing the mothers and frightening the babies.
He means well and just wants someone to play with.
But in our sanctuary corner of the woods, they can eat,
sleep and prance in peace. Just the way they like it.

God bless all creatures, in all their countless homes.
And the people who love them in their many ways.

Be Attitudes

Blessed are the children of Light,
for their hearts shine brightly.

Blessed are those who dedicate their lives to prayer,
for their prayers will be answered.

Blessed are the open minded,
for they shall not live in fear.

Blessed are those who hunger for Truth,
for it will be revealed to them.

Blessed are those who stand up to tyrants,
for they shall know freedom.

Blessed are those who perform humble deeds,
for their actions change the course of history.

Blessed are the peacemakers,
for they shall overcome struggle and live in peace.

Blessed are those who serve the children and elders,
for they are Masters in disguise.

Blessed are the grateful,
for they live in contentment.

Blessed are the jokesters,
for they bring smiles to everyone.

Blessed are the gardeners,
for they sow seeds of hope.

Blessed are the singers,
for they move hearts to great love.

Blessed are the Lovers,
for they express the essence of God.

Blessed are the Angel Ministers,
For they bring the messages of hope.

Blessed are the seekers of divinity,
for they shall create Heaven on earth.

Bucket List

Have you sincerely
written out all that is still
UNDONE?

A notebook full of places to see
like volcanoes forming lava rocks
or universes birthing stars?
Who wouldn't want to see them all?

What of the books to be read?
Children to see grow up?
Trails and bends around rivers
to be explored?
It's beyond understanding how
anyone
would leave voluntarily.

But there's something
about that mysterious bucket
that holds a measured amount
for each carrier
before it develops holes
or is easily knocked over
spilling sinew and bones,
fracturing hips and swelling ankles.

Quick! Look at your list!
Have you floated in a hot air balloon?
Rafted down the rapids?
Has life's bungee cord given you
enough upside-down thrills yet?
Grab onto it and ride it past the nebulas
where death cannot find you.

Never Saw It Coming?

In "War of the Worlds" fictional broadcast,
giant alien invaders were disabled
by the smallest of microbes,
for which they had no immunities.

So too the machinery of 2020 businesses,
the ships of war, factories, institutions,
schools, universities, parks and concerts
ground to a stop with fear of contagious virus.

Cracks and chasms opened in the structures
by which time and worth were measured,
unequally swallowing the vulnerable and poor.
Lives lost or forever altered. No hugs at funerals.

But light also beamed through those openings
as parents and children rediscovered each other
when they sought to work, study and live together.
As communities found their purpose in service.

New ways to communicate, to see each other,
alternatives to working in claustrophobic cubicles,
recognition of essential workers (that's everyone)
and glaring disparities in pay and working conditions.

Extended Time, to take off the blinders of routine
and listen to each other's wounds and joys.
Quiet of slower pace, planting a garden,
breathing in nature and rediscovering priorities.

Most of all, the spotlight on Oneness
of all humanity and the living environment,
refusing fear and extending LOVE.

Last Whispers To Paula
Beloved Friend and Teacher

Weave yourself into the tendrils
of my dreams, but don't leave me
without your soft smile.
Please, whisper poems in my ear.

Between the breeze and the twilight dew,
I can almost hear your sweet voice
coaxing me to write "more." But how can I,
without you, to understand the poems' joy?

I miss our tender friendship,
your gardens of wisdom so gently tended,
so kindly shared. Will I ever find you nodding
in blooming roses or in a sweet prayer?

You still have much to teach me,
now you've walked through the veil.
If I stand open like a lily and trust in the rain,
will I glimpse your light inviting me to heal?

Do you see colors in sunsets?
Is the earth more green or blue?
Do you speak in the music of words?
Or are songs of peace all around?

Dear sister, your every humble action
was "to show, not tell." Please comfort me
in the meadow of light, where the hum
of God's breath goes on, forever.

Acknowledgements

I was once introduced at a social gathering as a poet. One woman spoke to me for a few minutes and declared with great surprise, "You may be a poet, but you don't talk funny." I told her that though we may not talk funny, she might be surprised that poets often "think funny." Thanks to all who are willing to think in unique ways about the world and all our relationships, and have encouraged me to write mine down.

Great gratitude to all of you who know that I speak the language of my heart, both poignant and joyful. Thanks to my beloved husband of over fifty years (who also provided the photos in this book), our daughter, my dear sisters, extended family and many wonderful friends who read the first drafts, shared their feedback and came to the poetry readings, or had me read at their homes, weddings, memorials and life celebrations, especially Judith Coates, Kimberly Marooney, Pat Mawson, Jan Knutson, Ed Hutchinson, Shirley Blase, Kathy and Bill Evans, Marline and Doug Atterbury, as well as my former Seattle Writing Group and its late leader and mentor, the poet Paula Gardiner. I extend appreciation for my current Writing Group, Kathy See Kennedy, Al Kitching, Mark Schrader, Neal and Kathryn Fridley, and Kristine Roberton. All the instructors in the University of Washington's Poetry Writing certificate program who gave me advice and encouragement.

Thank you to my talented publishers – Heidi Hansen and Linda B. Myers of Olympic Peninsula Authors for their support and skill in producing this book of poetry. Great gratitude for hosting the Fourth Friday Readings forum for a community gathering place for authors to come together and read their work. You are all greatly appreciated for your generosity.

Thanks to the editors of the following journals and anthologies, where versions of the following poems appeared:

Prevail: Tackling Trouble Times in the Words of Olympic Peninsula Authors: "Never Saw It Coming"
In the Words of Olympic Peninsula Authors Vol. 3: "Jacaranda Tree", "On Writing Poetry", "Labyrinth", "Mama's Chicken Soup", "Morning After February Snowfall 2019" "Danger, Strong Current", "Danger, Strong Whirlpools"
In the Words of Olympic Peninsula Authors Vol. 2: "Aftermath Winter Storms on the Olympic Peninsula", "Astonishment", "Mists of the Mountains", "Autumn Snapshots", "Forest Magic-Mt. Pleasant Eternal July", "January Sounds Beneath the Silence, Mt. Pleasant Woods", "Lone Duck in Wetlands", "Spring – Then and Now", "Summer Reflections by Lake Creek"
Tidepools Journal 2020: "Wind at Kalaloch Beach"
Tidepools Journal 2017: "Rosebud"
Rainshadow Poetry: "A Hundred Thousand Things Forgotten"
Fluidity Art Exhibit 2020: "Heart of Lake Creek" photograph
Unity in the Olympics Newsletter: "Love has Chosen Us"
Wildwillow: Women's Anthology Project: "Carbon Glacier"
Wings to My Breath: "The Spiral Universe," "Crystal Hot Springs"
At the Edge of the Earth: "Blackberry Lover"

About The Author

Eva Maria (Jarosz) McGinnis was born in a refugee center in post WWII Germany. With her Polish parents, she immigrated to the United States when Eva was a young child. She grew up in Detroit in the 1950s and 60s along with her three sisters, within the Polish community. Fascinated with poetry at an early age, she was coached by her father to memorize and recite long poems. From her gentle mother, who cultivated both flower and vegetable gardens, Eva came to appreciate nature's beauty and bounty. As with most immigrant families, her parents stressed the importance of a good education.

An eager scholar, Eva graduated from Michigan State with a BA in English, then a Masters from Iowa State in Adult Education and Counseling Psychology. She and her husband moved to Washington State in 1980. In 1992, she completed a certificate program In Poetry from the University of Washington. Along the way, her career included teaching for Western Washington University, counseling at a vocational school, environmental and social activism at Iowa State University, and working as a training director and instructor at several non-profits. She also had her own counseling practice for several years. Throughout the work years, she kept up her writing by belonging to a women's writing group. Now she facilitates a group in her neighborhood. She is the mother of a professional dancer.

After fifty-plus years of employment, she and her husband moved into the next phase of their lives. They have an original glass art and jewelry business, Bead-Love-It.com. They can be found hiking, taking photos, and gathering mushrooms in their beloved Olympic Peninsula of Washington State. In 2020, they quietly celebrated 50 years of marriage as well. Eva also serves her spiritual communities as prayer chaplain, guest speaker and in other board capacities.

Eva McGinnis has written two books of poetry, **Wings to my Breath** and **At the Edge of the Earth,** and has had her work published in literary books and magazines, including **In the Words of Olympic Peninsula Authors Vol 2 & 3**, **Prevail Anthology**; **Tidepools** 2017 & 2020; **Rainshadow Poetry Anthology; Wild Willow Women's Anthology Project; Seattle Poems by Seattle Poets Anthology**; **Woman as Hero Anthology**; **A Mother's Touch**; **Spindrift** '93, '94 & '95, and has had her poems displayed on the Poetry Buses Program in Seattle. She can be reached at Evapoet@mcginnishome.org.

Nature always wears the colors of the spirit
Ralph Waldo Emerson

Made in the USA
Columbia, SC
12 November 2021

48666790R00058